Password notebook

Keep Track Books

A

Name	Date
Web address	
Username/login	
Password	PIN
Security questions/notes	

Name	Date
Web address	
Username/login	
Password	PIN
Security questions/notes	

Name	Date
Web address	
Username/login	
Password	PIN
Security questions/notes	

Name	Date
Web address	
Username/login	
Password	PIN
Security questions/notes	

Name	Date
Web address	
Username/login	
Password	PIN
Security questions/notes	

Name	Date
Web address	
Username/login	
Password	PIN
Security questions/notes	

A

Name	Date
Web address	
Username/login	
Password	PIN
Security questions/notes	

Name	Date
Web address	
Username/login	
Password	PIN
Security questions/notes	

Name	Date
Web address	
Username/login	
Password	PIN
Security questions/notes	

A

Name	Date
Web address	
Username/login	
Password	PIN
Security questions/notes	

Name	Date
Web address	
Username/login	
Password	PIN
Security questions/notes	

Name	Date
Web address	
Username/login	
Password	PIN
Security questions/notes	

B

Name	Date
Web address	
Username/login	
Password	PIN
Security questions/notes	

Name	Date
Web address	
Username/login	
Password	PIN
Security questions/notes	

Name	Date
Web address	
Username/login	
Password	PIN
Security questions/notes	

B

Name	Date
Web address	
Username/login	
Password	PIN
Security questions/notes	

Name	Date
Web address	
Username/login	
Password	PIN
Security questions/notes	

Name	Date
Web address	
Username/login	
Password	PIN
Security questions/notes	

Name	Date
Web address	
Username/login	
Password	PIN
Security questions/notes	

Name	Date
Web address	
Username/login	
Password	PIN
Security questions/notes	

Name	Date
Web address	
Username/login	
Password	PIN
Security questions/notes	

B

Name	Date
Web address	
Username/login	
Password	PIN
Security questions/notes	

Name	Date
Web address	
Username/login	
Password	PIN
Security questions/notes	

Name	Date
Web address	
Username/login	
Password	PIN
Security questions/notes	

C

Name	Date
Web address	
Username/login	
Password	PIN
Security questions/notes	

Name	Date
Web address	
Username/login	
Password	PIN
Security questions/notes	

Name	Date
Web address	
Username/login	
Password	PIN
Security questions/notes	

C

Name	Date
Web address	
Username/login	
Password	PIN
Security questions/notes	

Name	Date
Web address	
Username/login	
Password	PIN
Security questions/notes	

Name	Date
Web address	
Username/login	
Password	PIN
Security questions/notes	

C

Name	Date
Web address	
Username/login	
Password	PIN
Security questions/notes	

Name	Date
Web address	
Username/login	
Password	PIN
Security questions/notes	

Name	Date
Web address	
Username/login	
Password	PIN
Security questions/notes	

Name	Date
Web address	
Username/login	
Password	PIN
Security questions/notes	

Name	Date
Web address	
Username/login	
Password	PIN
Security questions/notes	

Name	Date
Web address	
Username/login	
Password	PIN
Security questions/notes	

D

Name	Date
Web address	
Username/login	
Password	PIN
Security questions/notes	

Name	Date
Web address	
Username/login	
Password	PIN
Security questions/notes	

Name	Date
Web address	
Username/login	
Password	PIN
Security questions/notes	

$$\boxed{\text{D}}$$

Name	Date
Web address	
Username/login	
Password	PIN
Security questions/notes	

Name	Date
Web address	
Username/login	
Password	PIN
Security questions/notes	

Name	Date
Web address	
Username/login	
Password	PIN
Security questions/notes	

D

Name	Date
Web address	
Username/login	
Password	PIN
Security questions/notes	

Name	Date
Web address	
Username/login	
Password	PIN
Security questions/notes	

Name	Date
Web address	
Username/login	
Password	PIN
Security questions/notes	

D	

Name	Date
Web address	
Username/login	
Password	PIN
Security questions/notes	

Name	Date
Web address	
Username/login	
Password	PIN
Security questions/notes	

Name	Date
Web address	
Username/login	
Password	PIN
Security questions/notes	

E

Name	Date

Web address	

Username/login	

Password	PIN

Security questions/notes

Name	Date

Web address	

Username/login	

Password	PIN

Security questions/notes

Name	Date

Web address	

Username/login	

Password	PIN

Security questions/notes

E

Name	Date
Web address	
Username/login	
Password	PIN
Security questions/notes	

Name	Date
Web address	
Username/login	
Password	PIN
Security questions/notes	

Name	Date
Web address	
Username/login	
Password	PIN
Security questions/notes	

E

Name	Date
Web address	
Username/login	
Password	PIN

Security questions/notes

Name	Date
Web address	
Username/login	
Password	PIN

Security questions/notes

Name	Date
Web address	
Username/login	
Password	PIN

Security questions/notes

E

Name	Date
Web address	
Username/login	
Password	PIN
Security questions/notes	

Name	Date
Web address	
Username/login	
Password	PIN
Security questions/notes	

Name	Date
Web address	
Username/login	
Password	PIN
Security questions/notes	

F

Name	Date
Web address	
Username/login	
Password	PIN
Security questions/notes	

Name	Date
Web address	
Username/login	
Password	PIN
Security questions/notes	

Name	Date
Web address	
Username/login	
Password	PIN
Security questions/notes	

<table>
<tr><td>F</td></tr>
</table>

Name	Date
Web address	
Username/login	
Password	PIN
Security questions/notes	

Name	Date
Web address	
Username/login	
Password	PIN
Security questions/notes	

Name	Date
Web address	
Username/login	
Password	PIN
Security questions/notes	

F

Name	Date
Web address	
Username/login	
Password	PIN
Security questions/notes	

Name	Date
Web address	
Username/login	
Password	PIN
Security questions/notes	

Name	Date
Web address	
Username/login	
Password	PIN
Security questions/notes	

F

Name	Date

Web address	

Username/login	

Password	PIN

Security questions/notes	

Name	Date

Web address	

Username/login	

Password	PIN

Security questions/notes	

Name	Date

Web address	

Username/login	

Password	PIN

Security questions/notes	

G

Name	Date
Web address	
Username/login	
Password	PIN
Security questions/notes	

Name	Date
Web address	
Username/login	
Password	PIN
Security questions/notes	

Name	Date
Web address	
Username/login	
Password	PIN
Security questions/notes	

Name	Date
Web address	
Username/login	
Password	PIN
Security questions/notes	

Name	Date
Web address	
Username/login	
Password	PIN
Security questions/notes	

Name	Date
Web address	
Username/login	
Password	PIN
Security questions/notes	

Name	Date
Web address	
Username/login	
Password	PIN
Security questions/notes	

Name	Date
Web address	
Username/login	
Password	PIN
Security questions/notes	

Name	Date
Web address	
Username/login	
Password	PIN
Security questions/notes	

| G |

Name	Date
Web address	
Username/login	
Password	PIN
Security questions/notes	

Name	Date
Web address	
Username/login	
Password	PIN
Security questions/notes	

Name	Date
Web address	
Username/login	
Password	PIN
Security questions/notes	

Name	Date
Web address	
Username/login	
Password	PIN
Security questions/notes	

Name	Date
Web address	
Username/login	
Password	PIN
Security questions/notes	

Name	Date
Web address	
Username/login	
Password	PIN
Security questions/notes	

| H | |

Name	Date
Web address	
Username/login	
Password	PIN
Security questions/notes	

Name	Date
Web address	
Username/login	
Password	PIN
Security questions/notes	

Name	Date
Web address	
Username/login	
Password	PIN
Security questions/notes	

H

Name	Date
Web address	
Username/login	
Password	PIN
Security questions/notes	

Name	Date
Web address	
Username/login	
Password	PIN
Security questions/notes	

Name	Date
Web address	
Username/login	
Password	PIN
Security questions/notes	

Name	Date
Web address	
Username/login	
Password	PIN
Security questions/notes	

Name	Date
Web address	
Username/login	
Password	PIN
Security questions/notes	

Name	Date
Web address	
Username/login	
Password	PIN
Security questions/notes	

1

Name	Date
Web address	
Username/login	
Password	PIN
Security questions/notes	

Name	Date
Web address	
Username/login	
Password	PIN
Security questions/notes	

Name	Date
Web address	
Username/login	
Password	PIN
Security questions/notes	

I		

Name		Date
Web address		
Username/login		
Password		PIN
Security questions/notes		

Name		Date
Web address		
Username/login		
Password		PIN
Security questions/notes		

Name		Date
Web address		
Username/login		
Password		PIN
Security questions/notes		

<table>
<tr><td>Name</td><td>Date</td></tr>
<tr><td colspan="2">Web address</td></tr>
<tr><td colspan="2">Username/login</td></tr>
<tr><td>Password</td><td>PIN</td></tr>
<tr><td colspan="2">Security questions/notes</td></tr>
</table>

<table>
<tr><td>Name</td><td>Date</td></tr>
<tr><td colspan="2">Web address</td></tr>
<tr><td colspan="2">Username/login</td></tr>
<tr><td>Password</td><td>PIN</td></tr>
<tr><td colspan="2">Security questions/notes</td></tr>
</table>

<table>
<tr><td>Name</td><td>Date</td></tr>
<tr><td colspan="2">Web address</td></tr>
<tr><td colspan="2">Username/login</td></tr>
<tr><td>Password</td><td>PIN</td></tr>
<tr><td colspan="2">Security questions/notes</td></tr>
</table>

I

Name	Date
Web address	
Username/login	
Password	PIN
Security questions/notes	

Name	Date
Web address	
Username/login	
Password	PIN
Security questions/notes	

Name	Date
Web address	
Username/login	
Password	PIN
Security questions/notes	

J

Name	Date
Web address	
Username/login	
Password	PIN
Security questions/notes	

Name	Date
Web address	
Username/login	
Password	PIN
Security questions/notes	

Name	Date
Web address	
Username/login	
Password	PIN
Security questions/notes	

J

Name	Date
Web address	
Username/login	
Password	PIN
Security questions/notes	

Name	Date
Web address	
Username/login	
Password	PIN
Security questions/notes	

Name	Date
Web address	
Username/login	
Password	PIN
Security questions/notes	

J

Name	Date
Web address	
Username/login	
Password	PIN
Security questions/notes	

Name	Date
Web address	
Username/login	
Password	PIN
Security questions/notes	

Name	Date
Web address	
Username/login	
Password	PIN
Security questions/notes	

| J | |

Name	Date
Web address	
Username/login	
Password	PIN
Security questions/notes	

Name	Date
Web address	
Username/login	
Password	PIN
Security questions/notes	

Name	Date
Web address	
Username/login	
Password	PIN
Security questions/notes	

K

Name	Date
Web address	
Username/login	
Password	PIN
Security questions/notes	

Name	Date
Web address	
Username/login	
Password	PIN
Security questions/notes	

Name	Date
Web address	
Username/login	
Password	PIN
Security questions/notes	

K

Name	Date
Web address	
Username/login	
Password	PIN
Security questions/notes	

Name	Date
Web address	
Username/login	
Password	PIN
Security questions/notes	

Name	Date
Web address	
Username/login	
Password	PIN
Security questions/notes	

K

Name	Date
Web address	
Username/login	
Password	PIN
Security questions/notes	

Name	Date
Web address	
Username/login	
Password	PIN
Security questions/notes	

Name	Date
Web address	
Username/login	
Password	PIN
Security questions/notes	

Name	Date
Web address	
Username/login	
Password	PIN
Security questions/notes	

Name	Date
Web address	
Username/login	
Password	PIN
Security questions/notes	

Name	Date
Web address	
Username/login	
Password	PIN
Security questions/notes	

L

Name	Date
Web address	
Username/login	
Password	PIN
Security questions/notes	

Name	Date
Web address	
Username/login	
Password	PIN
Security questions/notes	

Name	Date
Web address	
Username/login	
Password	PIN
Security questions/notes	

| L |

Name	Date
Web address	
Username/login	
Password	PIN
Security questions/notes	

Name	Date
Web address	
Username/login	
Password	PIN
Security questions/notes	

Name	Date
Web address	
Username/login	
Password	PIN
Security questions/notes	

L

Name	Date
Web address	
Username/login	
Password	PIN
Security questions/notes	

Name	Date
Web address	
Username/login	
Password	PIN
Security questions/notes	

Name	Date
Web address	
Username/login	
Password	PIN
Security questions/notes	

L

Name	Date

Web address	

Username/login	

Password	PIN

Security questions/notes

Name	Date

Web address	

Username/login	

Password	PIN

Security questions/notes

Name	Date

Web address	

Username/login	

Password	PIN

Security questions/notes

M

Name	Date
Web address	
Username/login	
Password	PIN
Security questions/notes	

Name	Date
Web address	
Username/login	
Password	PIN
Security questions/notes	

Name	Date
Web address	
Username/login	
Password	PIN
Security questions/notes	

M

Name	Date
Web address	
Username/login	
Password	PIN
Security questions/notes	

Name	Date
Web address	
Username/login	
Password	PIN
Security questions/notes	

Name	Date
Web address	
Username/login	
Password	PIN
Security questions/notes	

M

Name	Date
Web address	
Username/login	
Password	PIN
Security questions/notes	

Name	Date
Web address	
Username/login	
Password	PIN
Security questions/notes	

Name	Date
Web address	
Username/login	
Password	PIN
Security questions/notes	

| M |

Name	Date
Web address	
Username/login	
Password	PIN
Security questions/notes	

Name	Date
Web address	
Username/login	
Password	PIN
Security questions/notes	

Name	Date
Web address	
Username/login	
Password	PIN
Security questions/notes	

Name	Date
Web address	
Username/login	
Password	PIN
Security questions/notes	

Name	Date
Web address	
Username/login	
Password	PIN
Security questions/notes	

Name	Date
Web address	
Username/login	
Password	PIN
Security questions/notes	

Name	Date
Web address	
Username/login	
Password	PIN
Security questions/notes	

Name	Date
Web address	
Username/login	
Password	PIN
Security questions/notes	

Name	Date
Web address	
Username/login	
Password	PIN
Security questions/notes	

Name	Date
Web address	
Username/login	
Password	PIN
Security questions/notes	

Name	Date
Web address	
Username/login	
Password	PIN
Security questions/notes	

Name	Date
Web address	
Username/login	
Password	PIN
Security questions/notes	

N

Name	Date
Web address	
Username/login	
Password	PIN
Security questions/notes	

Name	Date
Web address	
Username/login	
Password	PIN
Security questions/notes	

Name	Date
Web address	
Username/login	
Password	PIN
Security questions/notes	

Name	Date
Web address	
Username/login	
Password	PIN
Security questions/notes	

Name	Date
Web address	
Username/login	
Password	PIN
Security questions/notes	

Name	Date
Web address	
Username/login	
Password	PIN
Security questions/notes	

Name	Date
Web address	
Username/login	
Password	PIN
Security questions/notes	

Name	Date
Web address	
Username/login	
Password	PIN
Security questions/notes	

Name	Date
Web address	
Username/login	
Password	PIN
Security questions/notes	

Name	Date

Web address

Username/login

Password	PIN

Security questions/notes

Name	Date

Web address

Username/login

Password	PIN

Security questions/notes

Name	Date

Web address

Username/login

Password	PIN

Security questions/notes

<table>
<tr><td>Name</td><td>Date</td></tr>
<tr><td colspan="2">Web address</td></tr>
<tr><td colspan="2">Username/login</td></tr>
<tr><td>Password</td><td>PIN</td></tr>
<tr><td colspan="2">Security questions/notes</td></tr>
</table>

<table>
<tr><td>Name</td><td>Date</td></tr>
<tr><td colspan="2">Web address</td></tr>
<tr><td colspan="2">Username/login</td></tr>
<tr><td>Password</td><td>PIN</td></tr>
<tr><td colspan="2">Security questions/notes</td></tr>
</table>

<table>
<tr><td>Name</td><td>Date</td></tr>
<tr><td colspan="2">Web address</td></tr>
<tr><td colspan="2">Username/login</td></tr>
<tr><td>Password</td><td>PIN</td></tr>
<tr><td colspan="2">Security questions/notes</td></tr>
</table>

<table>
<tr><td>P</td></tr>
</table>

Name	Date

Web address

Username/login

Password	PIN

Security questions/notes

Name	Date

Web address

Username/login

Password	PIN

Security questions/notes

Name	Date

Web address

Username/login

Password	PIN

Security questions/notes

| P | |

Name	Date
Web address	
Username/login	
Password	PIN
Security questions/notes	

Name	Date
Web address	
Username/login	
Password	PIN
Security questions/notes	

Name	Date
Web address	
Username/login	
Password	PIN
Security questions/notes	

P

Name	Date
Web address	
Username/login	
Password	PIN
Security questions/notes	

Name	Date
Web address	
Username/login	
Password	PIN
Security questions/notes	

Name	Date
Web address	
Username/login	
Password	PIN
Security questions/notes	

P

Name	Date
Web address	
Username/login	
Password	PIN
Security questions/notes	

Name	Date
Web address	
Username/login	
Password	PIN
Security questions/notes	

Name	Date
Web address	
Username/login	
Password	PIN
Security questions/notes	

Q

Name	Date
Web address	
Username/login	
Password	PIN
Security questions/notes	

Name	Date
Web address	
Username/login	
Password	PIN
Security questions/notes	

Name	Date
Web address	
Username/login	
Password	PIN
Security questions/notes	

Name	Date
Web address	
Username/login	
Password	PIN
Security questions/notes	

Name	Date
Web address	
Username/login	
Password	PIN
Security questions/notes	

Name	Date
Web address	
Username/login	
Password	PIN
Security questions/notes	

Q

Name	Date
Web address	
Username/login	
Password	PIN
Security questions/notes	

Name	Date
Web address	
Username/login	
Password	PIN
Security questions/notes	

Name	Date
Web address	
Username/login	
Password	PIN
Security questions/notes	

Q

Name	Date
Web address	
Username/login	
Password	PIN
Security questions/notes	

Name	Date
Web address	
Username/login	
Password	PIN
Security questions/notes	

Name	Date
Web address	
Username/login	
Password	PIN
Security questions/notes	

R

Name	Date
Web address	
Username/login	
Password	PIN
Security questions/notes	

Name	Date
Web address	
Username/login	
Password	PIN
Security questions/notes	

Name	Date
Web address	
Username/login	
Password	PIN
Security questions/notes	

R

Name	Date
Web address	
Username/login	
Password	PIN
Security questions/notes	

Name	Date
Web address	
Username/login	
Password	PIN
Security questions/notes	

Name	Date
Web address	
Username/login	
Password	PIN
Security questions/notes	

R

Name	Date
Web address	
Username/login	
Password	PIN
Security questions/notes	

Name	Date
Web address	
Username/login	
Password	PIN
Security questions/notes	

Name	Date
Web address	
Username/login	
Password	PIN
Security questions/notes	

R

Name	Date
Web address	
Username/login	
Password	PIN
Security questions/notes	

Name	Date
Web address	
Username/login	
Password	PIN
Security questions/notes	

Name	Date
Web address	
Username/login	
Password	PIN
Security questions/notes	

S

Name	Date
Web address	
Username/login	
Password	PIN
Security questions/notes	

Name	Date
Web address	
Username/login	
Password	PIN
Security questions/notes	

Name	Date
Web address	
Username/login	
Password	PIN
Security questions/notes	

S

Name	Date
Web address	
Username/login	
Password	PIN
Security questions/notes	

Name	Date
Web address	
Username/login	
Password	PIN
Security questions/notes	

Name	Date
Web address	
Username/login	
Password	PIN
Security questions/notes	

S

Name	Date
Web address	
Username/login	
Password	PIN
Security questions/notes	

Name	Date
Web address	
Username/login	
Password	PIN
Security questions/notes	

Name	Date
Web address	
Username/login	
Password	PIN
Security questions/notes	

S

Name	Date
Web address	
Username/login	
Password	PIN
Security questions/notes	

Name	Date
Web address	
Username/login	
Password	PIN
Security questions/notes	

Name	Date
Web address	
Username/login	
Password	PIN
Security questions/notes	

T

Name	Date
Web address	
Username/login	
Password	PIN
Security questions/notes	

Name	Date
Web address	
Username/login	
Password	PIN
Security questions/notes	

Name	Date
Web address	
Username/login	
Password	PIN
Security questions/notes	

T

Name	Date
Web address	
Username/login	
Password	PIN
Security questions/notes	

Name	Date
Web address	
Username/login	
Password	PIN
Security questions/notes	

Name	Date
Web address	
Username/login	
Password	PIN
Security questions/notes	

T

Name	Date
Web address	
Username/login	
Password	PIN
Security questions/notes	

Name	Date
Web address	
Username/login	
Password	PIN
Security questions/notes	

Name	Date
Web address	
Username/login	
Password	PIN
Security questions/notes	

T

Name	Date
Web address	
Username/login	
Password	PIN
Security questions/notes	

Name	Date
Web address	
Username/login	
Password	PIN
Security questions/notes	

Name	Date
Web address	
Username/login	
Password	PIN
Security questions/notes	

U

Name	Date
Web address	
Username/login	
Password	PIN
Security questions/notes	

Name	Date
Web address	
Username/login	
Password	PIN
Security questions/notes	

Name	Date
Web address	
Username/login	
Password	PIN
Security questions/notes	

Name	Date
Web address	
Username/login	
Password	PIN
Security questions/notes	

Name	Date
Web address	
Username/login	
Password	PIN
Security questions/notes	

Name	Date
Web address	
Username/login	
Password	PIN
Security questions/notes	

U

Name	Date

Web address

Username/login

Password	PIN

Security questions/notes

Name	Date

Web address

Username/login

Password	PIN

Security questions/notes

Name	Date

Web address

Username/login

Password	PIN

Security questions/notes

U

Name	Date
Web address	
Username/login	
Password	PIN
Security questions/notes	

Name	Date
Web address	
Username/login	
Password	PIN
Security questions/notes	

Name	Date
Web address	
Username/login	
Password	PIN
Security questions/notes	

V

Name	Date
Web address	
Username/login	
Password	PIN
Security questions/notes	

Name	Date
Web address	
Username/login	
Password	PIN
Security questions/notes	

Name	Date
Web address	
Username/login	
Password	PIN
Security questions/notes	

Name	Date
Web address	
Username/login	
Password	PIN
Security questions/notes	

Name	Date
Web address	
Username/login	
Password	PIN
Security questions/notes	

Name	Date
Web address	
Username/login	
Password	PIN
Security questions/notes	

V

Name	Date
Web address	
Username/login	
Password	PIN
Security questions/notes	

Name	Date
Web address	
Username/login	
Password	PIN
Security questions/notes	

Name	Date
Web address	
Username/login	
Password	PIN
Security questions/notes	

V	

Name	Date
Web address	
Username/login	
Password	PIN
Security questions/notes	

Name	Date
Web address	
Username/login	
Password	PIN
Security questions/notes	

Name	Date
Web address	
Username/login	
Password	PIN
Security questions/notes	

W

Name	Date
Web address	
Username/login	
Password	PIN
Security questions/notes	

Name	Date
Web address	
Username/login	
Password	PIN
Security questions/notes	

Name	Date
Web address	
Username/login	
Password	PIN
Security questions/notes	

Name	Date
Web address	
Username/login	
Password	PIN
Security questions/notes	

Name	Date
Web address	
Username/login	
Password	PIN
Security questions/notes	

Name	Date
Web address	
Username/login	
Password	PIN
Security questions/notes	

W

Name	Date
Web address	
Username/login	
Password	PIN
Security questions/notes	

Name	Date
Web address	
Username/login	
Password	PIN
Security questions/notes	

Name	Date
Web address	
Username/login	
Password	PIN
Security questions/notes	

Name	Date
Web address	
Username/login	
Password	PIN
Security questions/notes	

Name	Date
Web address	
Username/login	
Password	PIN
Security questions/notes	

Name	Date
Web address	
Username/login	
Password	PIN
Security questions/notes	

[X]

Name	Date
Web address	
Username/login	
Password	PIN
Security questions/notes	

Name	Date
Web address	
Username/login	
Password	PIN
Security questions/notes	

Name	Date
Web address	
Username/login	
Password	PIN
Security questions/notes	

X	

Name	Date
Web address	
Username/login	
Password	PIN
Security questions/notes	

Name	Date
Web address	
Username/login	
Password	PIN
Security questions/notes	

Name	Date
Web address	
Username/login	
Password	PIN
Security questions/notes	

Y

Name	Date
Web address	
Username/login	
Password	PIN
Security questions/notes	

Name	Date
Web address	
Username/login	
Password	PIN
Security questions/notes	

Name	Date
Web address	
Username/login	
Password	PIN
Security questions/notes	

| Y |

Name	Date
Web address	
Username/login	
Password	PIN
Security questions/notes	

Name	Date
Web address	
Username/login	
Password	PIN
Security questions/notes	

Name	Date
Web address	
Username/login	
Password	PIN
Security questions/notes	

Y

Name	Date
Web address	
Username/login	
Password	PIN
Security questions/notes	

Name	Date
Web address	
Username/login	
Password	PIN
Security questions/notes	

Name	Date
Web address	
Username/login	
Password	PIN
Security questions/notes	

Y

Name	Date
Web address	
Username/login	
Password	PIN
Security questions/notes	

Name	Date
Web address	
Username/login	
Password	PIN
Security questions/notes	

Name	Date
Web address	
Username/login	
Password	PIN
Security questions/notes	

Z

Name	Date
Web address	
Username/login	
Password	PIN
Security questions/notes	

Name	Date
Web address	
Username/login	
Password	PIN
Security questions/notes	

Name	Date
Web address	
Username/login	
Password	PIN
Security questions/notes	

Z

Name	Date
Web address	
Username/login	
Password	PIN
Security questions/notes	

Name	Date
Web address	
Username/login	
Password	PIN
Security questions/notes	

Name	Date
Web address	
Username/login	
Password	PIN
Security questions/notes	

Keep Track Books brings you
a variety of essential notebooks —
including password books
with the same interior as this one,
but in different sizes and
with different cover designs.

Search for 'Keep Track Books' on Amazon
or visit www.lusciousbooks.co.uk
to discover more notebooks.

Made in the USA
Monee, IL
07 July 2026